Lake Como

Itineraries and photographs of Lario, Ceresio and surrounding valleys

Lariologo

Photographs:
Aldo Nicoli
Marino Nicoli
Carlo Pozzoni

Graphic and page layout:
Marino Nicoli

Printer:
Tipografia Banfi s.r.l. - Como

Printing completed
in March 2010

Translation:
Chiedza K. Joseph

Thanks to Monica Neroni

*T*his guide is designed to accompany you and facilitate your discovery as you visit the scenic and artistic beauties of our lake.

To this end, five basic itineraries have been selected that clearly indicate the trails to follow and the monuments that you will meet along the way. For each itinerary there is a brief but comprehensive description which includes the history, main characteristics and the most significant features of each location. The only thing you will not find are technical details which, in any case, defeat the purpose of this easy to follow guide and our quest for simplicity.

The text is accompanied by more than 110 images to help you identify the locations and monuments described. It will also serve as a printed resource for you to keep as a compliment to the memories gathered during your vacation and stored in a keen mind and treasured by a sensitive spirit.

ITINERARIES

Como and the west side of the lake up to the Pian di Spagna

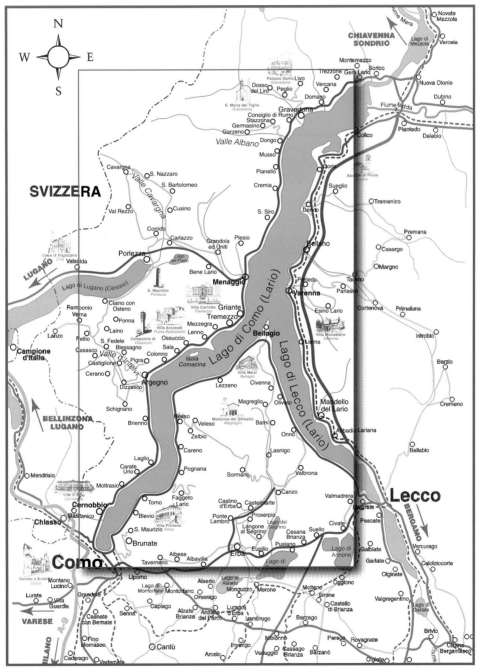

Side: the fountain at Villa Carlotta

O ur first itinerary starts in **Como**, a splendid and fascinating city full of history situated at the foot of the west branch of the Lario. Como was founded by the Romans in 59 BC with the name "Novum Comum" and to this day is the site of a magnificent town centre and a pedestrian zone surrounded and protected by powerful walls.

Piazza Cavour

We begin our stroll in **Piazza Cavour**, the ancient city port that was substituted at the end of the 1800's by a modern square facing the water. The boats and ferries that cut through the waters to reach the lakeside towns leave from here daily. Just a few steps will lead you to **Piazza del Duomo**, home to several interesting buildings. The **Broletto** is an elegant construction with a tricolour marble facade erected in the middle ages (13th century) as the Town Hall also known as the "Palazzo della Ragione" (Building of Reason). The stone bell tower on the left of the building was completed in the same century.

Next to the "Broletto" the magnificent mole of the "Duomo", the town cathedral, stands out. Formerly the site of the early Christian Church of Santa Maria Maggiore, work on the making of the Duomo began in 1396. It took nearly 400 years to complete this project which encompasses elements of the diverse architectural styles that characterised that long period of time: austere Gothic; elegant Renaissance; precious Baroque. The white facade in marble from Musso is a real masterpiece. Many artists worked on the building but without a doubt the greatest contribution was made by the Rodari brothers. These skilled sculptors are credited with the beau-

The Duomo and Broletto

tiful pair of podiums that frame the statues of Pliny the Younger (on the right) and Pliny the Elder (on the left) both illustrious citizens of Como in Roman times. Of particular interest are the sculptures of the lunettes over the portals and the five statues above the main entrance. In the centre is the Virgin Mary to whom the cathedral is dedicated and on her left is the statue of Sant'Abbondio the fourth bishop of Como and patron saint of the town. The rose window is certainly a gem with its splendid mosaics that capture your glance leading it up to the bold steeple.

The interior of the church is full of masterpieces. The wide naves host precious altars, stupendous tapestries and pictorial works of great value. The imposing cupola, designed by the Sicilian architect Juvarra was completed in 1744.

Behind the Duomo the Neoclassical facade of the **Teatro Sociale,** constructed in 1800 on the remains of the castle of the "Torre Rotonda" (The Round Tower), stands out with its Corinthian columns. Beyond the railway there is the Piazza del Popolo with the famous building formerly known as the **"Casa del Fascio" ("House of Fascism").** This building, erected in the 1930's and designed by the architect Giuseppe Terragni of Como, is universally considered to be a masterpiece of Rationalism.

In the heart of the old town you will encounter the medieval square **Piazza San Fedele,** formerly called the "Piazza del mercato del grano" (Grain Market Square). It owes its current name to the basilica situated here that was erected in the 10th century on the remains of an early Christian church dedicated to Santa Eufemia. It is a magnificent example of the Romanesque style Como is so famous for all over Europe. The Comacini Masters, extremely talented artisans native to the province of Como, built this temple with the simplicity and severity so characteristic of their style using local stone from Moltrasio. The most interesting part faces Via Vittorio Emanuele and has not undergone any renovations. It has got an ornate apse with a single doorway and a splendid pointed arch decorated with antique sculptures. Also in Piazza San Fedele there are two characteristic houses from the 16th century that bear testimony to the civil building style of that age.

At the end of the old town there is the imposing **Porta Torre**, the ancient entrance to the walled city built in the 12th century along with the surrounding walls that, to this day, protect the historic town centre. It was Federico Barbarossa who had it built to replace the previous defence system dating back to Roman times and destroyed by the Milanese at the end of the bloody "ten-year-war" which spelled defeat for the Larian city in 1127. We probably also have to credit the same Federico Barbarossa with the construction of the **Castello Baradello** that stands atop the hill of the same name of which only the tower and part of the wall remain. The strategic position of this fortress is really impressive as enemies could be made out from a distance.

Not far from the Porta Torre there is the Piazza Medaglie d'Oro Comasche. In this square there are two elegant buildings: Palazzo Giovio, now home of the **Museo Civico ed Archeologico**, and Palazzo Olginati that hosts the museum dedicated to Giuseppe Garibaldi. There are other museums in Como of great interest such as the **Civiche Raccolte d'Arte** and the Pinacoteca or Picture Gallery in the old Palazzo Volpi. Outside the city walls there is the one-of-

Former "House of Fascism"; inside the Basilica of S. Abbondio, the Basilica of S. Fedele and the Tempio Voltiano

P 15:
Villa
Olmo

a-kind **Museo della Seta,** where it is possible to follow the silk-making process, from the silk worm to the creation of this precious fabric.

Beyond the periphery of the city walls, along the old road or Via Regina, you can admire the **Basilica of S. Abbondio** which was once the cathedral of the city. It was built in the 11th century by Benedictine monks encompassing the existing apostolic basilica of Santi Pietro e Paolo. It is a magnificent example of Romanesque style in grey stone with a peculiarity: it has got two bell towers. The inside is wonderful in its simplicity and the columns, like stone trees, draw your attention to the frescoes on the apse. These murals are considered to be one of the most interesting pictorial cycles of the 1300's. The name of the artist known as the "Maestro di S. Abbondio" remains a mystery but the beauty of his work leaves one speechless to this very day.

Back toward the lake, near the public gardens, there are three other important works. The **Monumento alla Resistenza Europeo** inaugurated in 1983 by the President of the Republic at the time, Sandro Pertini, the **Monumento ai Caduti** built with slabs of stone from Carso and the building called **Novocomum**. The latter two are works of the aforementioned Rationalist architect Giuseppe Terragni.

Just beyond, almost directly on the water, sits the **Tempio Voltiano**, a charming construction in Neoclassical style. It was donated to the city in 1927 on the occasion of the centennial of the death of **Alessandro Volta**. Volta is certainly one of the most illustrious citizens of the capital of Lario born in 1745. In 1799 this famous scientist invented the electric battery and soon his fame spread beyond Italian borders.

A brief panoramic promenade with stupendous patrician villas will take you to the most famous dwelling of Como: **Villa Olmo** in pure Neoclassical style. The villa owes its name to a large tree, an elm, that originally grew within the magnificent park. This grand villa, designed by the architect Simone Cantoni, currently belongs to the town administration and is used to host prestigious exhibits and shows. The view from here is truly awesome.

In the distance you can make out the cupola of the Duomo and directly in front of you is Brunate hill. Along the slope you will note the tracks of the **Funicular**. This pleasant little train has been running since the end of the 1800's and today, in merely 8 minutes,

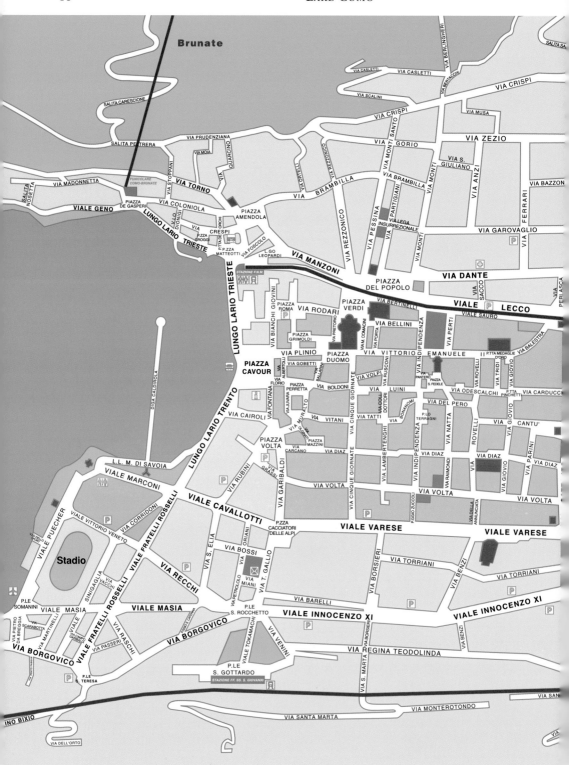

you can reach the village of **Brunate**. This is a panoramic location of rare beauty at an altitude of about 800 metres.

From the top you can easily discern the "castrum", namely the rectangle that made up the ancient Roman city plan, and then you can see the first basin of the lake with its numerous villas. You can even see the plains that lead to Milan.

Our itinerary now proceeds by car along the west shore of the lake to encounter the most panoramic and interesting sites along the way.

To get to Menaggio from Como, drive along the state road Via Regina which corresponds to the Roman Via Regia. From Milan, this ancient main road passed through Como leading to Chiavenna and eventually across the Spluga mountain pass to the Upper Rein and Danube.

Leave Como by Via Borgovico. After Tavernola turn left and drive along the new panoramic carriage road that flows easily. It passes mid-coast along the mountain just skimming the upper part of the little lakeside centres. The old and the new roads run parallel at different altitudes and merge just after the village of Laglio.

If you do not have much time at your disposal and you wish to reach the upper lake quickly then we suggest you take the panoramic road and follow the "the upper itinerary". However, if you have the time it is worth your while to take the lower road and follow the "lower itinerary".

Upper itinerary. Turn left and follow the signs for **Menaggio**, **Chiavenna**, **Sondrio** and you will immediately enter a tunnel that is 2.4 kilometres long. You will go through another three short tunnels. From this height above the lake you can enjoy magnificent sights. On the right there is a beautiful panorama of the promontory of the town of Torno situated on the opposite shore. Toward the end of the road, also on the opposite side, there is a wide view of Villa Pliniana, built right on the shore of the lake, isolated and immersed in the surrounding greenery. You will arrive at Torriggia, a hamlet of Laglio, where the roads of the upper and the lower itineraries meet.

Lower itinerary. After **Cernobbio** resume the principal itinerary and continue along the road that proceeds past parks and villas until **Moltrasio**. This village, which owes its name to a local grey-blue stone traditionally used in Como for construction, is a pleasant location much appreciated by tourists. From the road you will see the

P 16:
Plan of
Como

Pp 18
and 19:
Cernobbio

grand gateway to **Villa Passalacqua** on the left with an Italian styled terraced park surrounded by arches and walls. It has got a 19th century chapel with medieval sculptures.

After Moltrasio pass through **Carate Urio**. Here, at the beginning of the town, there is a villa from the 1700's called "Il Castello" ("The Castle") that currently belongs to Opus Dei. The road continues to **Laglio** where there is the pyramid shaped funeral monument of Giuseppe Franck (19th century), son of a famous German doctor, next to the cemetery. Then there is **Torriggia** which is the narrowest part of the lake measuring 650 metres.

Just beyond the town, the lower road merges with the upper road and proceeds to **Brienno**. Before the residential area there is a tunnel (1'150 metres) that you can take to avoid passing through the village itself. However, you might as well go along the narrow road that leads past the homes of this characteristic medieval village built along the slopes of the mountain interwoven with alleys and stairways. This parish has conserved for centuries relics of "San" Federico

P 20:
Villa
d'Este
and
Villa
d'Erba

Villa
Oleandra
in Laglio

Barbarossa the German leader responsible for the destruction of Milan and ferocious battles raged throughout Lombardy. However, his alliance with the people of Como during their battle against Milan is the reason for his "sainthood". At the end of the village there is a tunnel and above, on the right, the Church of the "Madonna Immacolata" on the rock spur.

A short stretch will take you to the wide inlet of **Argegno** from where the carriageway for Lanzo Intelvi branches off. At Argegno the lake reaches its maximum depth of 410 metres. Here the Regina state road surpasses the Telo stream (notice the medieval bridge on the left) and just a little way after the turn-off for the **Intelvi Valley** on the left there is the station for the funicular that, in just 4 minutes, travels to a height of 540 metres to reach the village of **Pigra**.

Then there is **Colonno** where the territory of the old "**Pieve dell'Isola Comacina**" (**The Parish of Comancina Island**) begins that proceeds until Ossuccio, then to **Tremezzina** and finally to Cadenabbia. The two territories extend on an 8-kilometre-long stretch of coast and is famous for its mild climate even in winter months.

The first village you encounter in the territory of the old "Island Parish" is **Sala Comacina**, situated directly opposite **Comacina Island**. It is the only island in the lake which can be reached in just a few minutes by a private boat service. The island, which is home to many archaeological remains, is about 600 metres long and has a perimeter of 2 kilometres.

In 1917 it was bequeathed to Alberto I, King of Belgium, who in turn donated it to the Italian government. It has been entrusted to the Academy of Fine Arts in Milan. On June 24 (St. John's day) or the following weekend, should the date fall on a weekday, a large festival is held. This popular event accompanied by a fire works display is very exciting.

In the middle ages this populated village was so wealthy it was called the "City of Gold". During the ten-year war between Como and Milan this well fortified village sided with the latter. The war ended in favour of the Milanese and marked destruction for Como. Then along came Barbarossa razing Milan to the ground and his allies, the people of Como, deemed it an appropriate time to vindicate themselves of the humiliation and damage suffered at the hands of the winners of the battle thirty years prior. In 1159 the island was razed to the ground and its inhabitants sought refuge along the nearby river banks, the majority of them moving to Varenna on the west side.

The locals call the quiet body of water cradled between the island and the river bank **"Zoca de l'oli" (an expression in the local dialect that means "basin of oil")**. This is not merely a pet name but refers to the cultivation of olives that the mild climate here allows for. This is a natural phenomenon that can be noted all along the southern strip of the Lario (Bellagio and Varenna).

Just a little further ahead is **Ospedaletto**, in the town of **Ossuccio**,

with its lovely Romanesque bell tower dating back to the 9th century. In the 1400's a late-Gothic cell was added on top of the bell tower. It belongs to the Church of Santa Maria Maddalena that was once part of a medieval hospice (to which the location, Ospedaletto, owes its name) which would receive pilgrims on their way to the Monastery of San Benedetto above. This Romanesque basilica can only be reached on foot and is about a two-and-a-half-hour walk along a mountain trial.

Above Ospedaletto there is Ossuccio which can be reached by leaving the main road and taking another road next to the bell tower that rises toward the mountain. Ossuccio is at the foot of an uphill road with 14 chapels that leads to the Baroque Sanctuary of the **Madonna del Soccorso** built in 1537. Along this avenue of chapels, that is about 1 kilometre long (half an hour on foot), 14 little tem-

Sala Comacina

Pp 24 and 25: Comacina Island and the bell tower in Ossuccio

The path to the Sanctuary of the Madonna del Soccorso and one of the chapels

ples built around a central plan between 1635 and 1714 are lined up. They contain groups of sculptures in painted terracotta, stuccoes and frescoes that depict the mysteries of the rosary. The 15th mystery is represented in the sanctuary. Of particular interest are chapels X,

XIII and XIV. Monte Sacro with its fourteen chapels has been declared a UNESCO world heritage site. This isolated sanctuary in a beautiful and panoramic position on the mountainside surrounded by lawns, olive trees and woods overlooks the island below as well as Tremezzo, Bellagio and Varenna. The interior is decorated with stuccoes, frescoes and staggered panels. The main altar completed in 1740 dominates along with the rich Baroque balustrade of the alter on the left. The floor laid in 1655 is made of marble from the lake. The 18th century organ is of carved wood. The fresco depicting the Madonna and child with Santa Eufemia dates back to 1501. The canvass with San Giuseppe is from the late 1800's and until 1963 was on display on an altar in the basilica of the Vatican. It was later donated to this sanctuary by Pope Giovanni XXIII and placed on the side altar.

More seasoned walkers may want to continue their journey and head toward the Abbey of San Benedetto. It is another two hours along a path that is quite steep at the beginning. The 9th century abbey was once part of a Benedictine Cluniac monastery of which remains little to no trace at all. The church, however, is very well preserved and is one of the oldest monumental examples of Romanesque architecture in Como.

At this point you can return to the lake and resume the original itinerary to reach the next village called Campo which is a hamlet of Lenno. On the promontory of Balbianello, far from the main road, is **Villa Balbianello** which was built in 1790 by Cardinal Durini upon the remains of a monastery. In addition to the two residential buildings, the complex includes a triple arcade, an old church and a magnificent little colonnade decorated with statues and stone balustrades. When the property belonged to Count Porro Lambertenghi, Silvio Pellico was the tutor and stayed here until his arrest and deportation to Spielberg. The property was passed on to Marquis Arconti and later to Guido Monzino a famous explorer and art collector. Today the villa belongs to the Italian Foundation for the Environment (FAI). The spacious park can be visited in summer (from March to October). You can reach this location by the carriageway or directly via the lake.

At **Lenno** you will find an interesting Romanesque baptistery with an octagonal base which sides feature pilasters and semi-columns. In the nearby Church of Santo Stefano the trapezoidal crypt with vaults supported by columns adorned by Carolingian (8th

Pp from 28 to 34: Villa Balbianello

century) and Comacini capitals is interesting. This monumental complex is situated below on the right side of the road. Before the church on the left, signs indicate an easy road that will take you to the plateau of the **Abbey of Acquafredda** less than a kilometre away. This monastery currently run by Capuchin monks was built in the 12th century but contains little or no trace of that period. The Abbey's name, "cold water", derives from a cool spring situated near the churchyard that is still active to this day. From this location you can reach the Abbey of San Benedetto by means of a road that is much more comfortable than the one that leaves from the Sanctuary of the Madonna del Soccorso. In any case, the travel time of about 2 hours is the same for both roads.

Proceeding along you will arrive at **Mezzegra**. Here, in **Giulino** to be precise, **Benito Mussolini** and Claretta Petacci were shot by Colonel Valerio on April 28, 1945 in front of the gate of number 14 Via XXIV Maggio, a road that rises from the lake to the mountain. The room in the house of Giacomo Di Maria in 4 Via Riale, where these prisoners of the partisans spent their last night, has remained intact.

Back on the state road a little ahead you will encounter **Bolvedro** with the monumental **Villa "La quiete"** from the 1700's. Parini, tutor of the Serbelloni home, spent 9 years here where he wrote part of "Mattino".

After there is **Tremezzo**, a famous tourist centre that has hosted celebrity personalities such as Giuseppe Verdi, Queen Victoria, Kaiser Wilhelm II and Chancellor Konrad Adenauer, just to name a few.

About 50 metres past the parish church the road veers off to the left toward **Rogaro**. After about a kilometre you will reach this village in the hamlet of Tremezzo that is known for its "vine asparagus" festival. It is also famous for the "Black Madonna" that is believed to have been brought here by refugees from Einsiedeln, Switzerland. To find it you have to park near the "Bel Sit" restaurant then walk past it, through a tiny gate, under a portico to the small square of the little church. Along the road to Rogaro there is a magnificent view of the lake and of Bellagio on the opposite side.

Once again on the main road, proceed along this coastal road accompanied by a beautiful promenade of porticoes to get to the entrance of **Villa Carlotta** atop a series of stairways (open from March to October). It was built as a country home around 1690 by Mar-

*Pp 36
and 37:
Tremezzo*

quis Giorgio Clerici. This Milanese banker decorated it with wonderful painted ceilings in Lombard-Baroque style and installed an Italian styled garden with stairways, a balustrade, the fountain and the waterfall of the dwarfs. In 1795 the villa was sold to Marquis Gianbattista Sommariva, a businessman from the Napoleonic era. This new owner brought the villa to the height of its splendour, enriching it with works of art. In 1834 the property was passed on to princess Marianna of Nassau, wife of Albert of Prussia, who gave it to her daughter Carlotta (to whom the villa owes its name) upon her marriage to the crown prince of Saxony-Meiningen. This last owner is accredited with the extension of the grounds and the addition of the English styled garden that the villa is famous for the world over. Since 1927 the villa has been state owned and is run by the independent board of Villa Carlotta.

Pp from 38 to 45: Villa Carlotta

Among the works of art of special interest is the group of marble statues from the school of Canova sculpted by the master's favourite pupil Tadolini. Also of interest is the statue *Palamede*, reconstructed by Canova, piece by piece, after it was shattered. Not to mention the large frieze *Trionfo di Alessandro Magno in Babilonia (The Triumph of Alexander the Great in Babylon) by* Bertel Thorvaldsen commissioned by Napoleon in 1811-12 and later bought by Count Sommariva for his home in Tremezzo. In what is called the room of chalk, among other things, you can admire sketches, reliefs and models of the arch of peace in Milan by Acquisti and Pacetti (1815). The various paintings by **Hayez** in the villa include the famous *Ultimo bacio di Giulietta e Romeo (Romeo and Juliette's last kiss)*. The furniture by Maggiolini, priceless tapestries along with Princess Carlotta's original furnishings are all very valuable.

Pp 42 and 43 clockwise: Amore e Psiche, Palamede, Carlotta's room and the central hall

Of course it is not possible to describe all of

the works of art housed in this sumptuous residence. In fact we must give due attention to the luxuriant garden for which Villa Carlotta is most famous. It is especially lush in spring with its dazzling display of azaleas and rhododendrons in bloom. Thanks to the exceptional climate on this part of the lake, within this immense park you can admire a botanical heritage of over five hundred species of trees and flowers. Among the plants of special interest there are a giant sequoia tree, cork trees, camphor, myrrh as well as papyrus and banana plants. The citrus pergola is always admired with oranges, mandarins, grapefruits, citrons, lemons and bergamots. The architectural plan of this

garden that wisely makes good use of the natural terrain is also very interesting.

Following a seemingly never ending string of houses you will

The Church of San Martino with Bellagio in the background reach **Cadenabbia**, with its rich 19th century villas and numerous hotels. An excursion to the Church of **San Martino** situated on a terrace of the steep "Sasso San Martino" offers an interesting view. You can get there by first taking a carriageway just past **Griante** to a bridge from where you have to proceed on foot for about 45 minutes. Beyond Cadenabbia the panorama is much more vast. Actually, at this point the lake reaches its maximum width (4.3 kilometres). On the right there is Villa Giuseppina, where Giuseppe Verdi used to stay as a guest of the Ricordi publishing house.

Now there is **Menaggio** at the mouth of the Menaggina valley that joins the Lario to the Ceresio. At the traffic lights where the town begins, follow the signs for the Menaggio town centre. Here there is a well known tourist centre with excellent hotel facilities, a golf course, a small tourist harbour, a campsite, a pool and a youth hostel. During the period immediately following the Second World War, this was a location appreciated by Winston Churchill who featured it in his paintings. On some of the houses in the medieval town you can see the remains of decorations from that period. In the heart of the town there is the historical centre with a square on the lake surrounded by bars and restaurants that is truly a gem. The beautiful lakeshore shaded by a string of trees at this point breaks

Pp from 47 to 49: Menaggio

away from the tourist harbour and reconnects with the state road, Via Regina. From here you can continue toward Nobiallo, a hamlet of Menaggio. The leaning Romanesque bell tower of the 13th century is very characteristic. On the road above you can see the Sanctuary of the Madonna della Pace erected in 1659 to celebrate the "Peace of the Pyreneans" who brought an end to the 30-year war between the French and the Spanish, who in these parts were both the conquerors and the conquered.

After a series of tunnels, which have greatly improved this route, and past Acquaseria you will arrive at **Santa Maria Rezzonico** a hamlet of the town of San Siro. The state road no longer passes through the inhabited town but you can catch sight of a castle that has since

Santa Maria Rezzonico   been transformed into a hotel. It was the dwelling of the Della Torre family, the landlords from 1360. The Venetian branch of this family tree lists among its descendents Pope Clemente XIII, but few recall that as a Cardinal he went by the name Gaetano Della Torre also known as Rezzonico. In fact, his great grandfather emigrated to Venice from this very town.

From this spot, continue along the old state road Via Regina. As you head toward Dongo you will pass Cremia and Pianello del Lario as well as Musso which is known for the caves where the stone used for the construction of numerous monuments such as the Duomo in Como and the Arch of Peace in Milano is mined. Finally at the end of a tunnel you will reach the gulf of **Dongo**. On the very lakeshore of this town, on April 28, 1945, the fascist leaders who had been caught the day before by partisans somewhere between Musso and Dongo were executed. They had attempted to escape along with Mussolini and Petacci to Switzerland. The latter two fugitives had been caught earlier and were held within the Neoclassical Palazzo Manzi in the main square of the town, currently home of

the town hall. Inside the building there is the gorgeous great hall called the "Sala doro" ("Golden Hall") where well-to-do families would host lavish parties. Today you can visit it during the business hours of the municipal offices. There is also a chapel and a library.

Dongo

Dongo, along with **Gravedona** and **Sorico**, once made up the **"Comunità delle Tre Pievi"** ("Community of the three parishes") which maintained a certain level of independence up until the end of the year 1100.

Above the town of Dongo is **Stazzona** which is known for its grottos and for the food festival that takes place here in August. From the road leading to Stazzona there are beautiful views of the plains

Gravedona   of Dongo and of the opposite shore toward the small lake in **Piona** and of the famous convent there. The parish church here is the first of a series of churches that call to mind Sicily, especially Palermo and Santa Rosalia. Actually, in centuries past, especially from the 16th to the 19th centuries, the people of this upper lake valley were forced to emigrate due to great poverty. Many chose Sicily where they became wholesale wine, or even communion wafer merchants. In Palermo immigrants from the Lario got together and formed fraternities or societies named after the saints of their parish churches back home. These societies not only had the function of maintaining ties with the homeland but would also come to the aid of its members in need. This assistance included helping the sick and the poor, intervening to free those in debt, standing bail for prisoners and furnishing dowries for brides-to-be as well as future nuns. With the rise of the fraternity in Palermo there also sprung an association back home called the "Schola Panormi" which had to manage the assets of the parish, the transfer of monies and donations of precious metals. To this day you can find numerous things that testify to the close rapport between the "Comunità delle Tre Pievi" and Palermo. Once again on the state road, near the intersection, you will find the Sanctuary of the Madonna delle Lacrime with an annexed monastery of Lesser Franciscan monks.

Once you leave Dongo you will travel through lush plains with vineyards all the way to **Gravedona**. At the beginning of the town follow the signs to the pier to the beautiful Church of **Santa Maria del Tiglio**.

Church of Santa Maria del Tiglio

Situated near the lake, it is a celebrated example of Roman-Lombard architecture built in the 12th century. It is open to visitors everyday from 9 a.m. to 6 p.m. Originally it was the baptistery of the parish that was the heart of Gravedona and the fresco of the apse bears testimony to the fact that it was dedicated to San Giovanni. The perimeter of the original building was rebuilt and there are still fragments of the mosaic floor that dates back to the 5th century, merely a century following official recognition of Christianity by Constantine spelling the end of persecution. The baptistery was demolished by the people of Gravedona during the overwhelming flourish of Romanesque style. Thus the building, as we see it today, only dates back to the 12th century. The black and white striped exterior is characterised by a massive bell tower erected right at the centre of the facade. Some mouldings and sculptures from the old baptistery have been incorporated into the facade. The interior wins you over with its strong lines and a single nave dominated by a large wooden crucifix from the 12th century situated above the small altar. In the centre, just below the new floor an incision gives an indication of the shape and size of the original baptismal immersion pool. On the walls there are remains of paintings. On the counter facade there is the *Giudizio universale* ("Universal Judgement", 14th century) and in the left apse three portraits depicting *Madonna and child, Sant'Anna* and *San Giuliano* from the 12th century. There are also the remains of the floor mosaic of the old baptistery and near the niche in the wall on the right there is a Roman alter. Above there is a women's gallery. Next to Santa Maria del Tiglio rises the parish

Palazzo Gallio

church which is a Baroque remodelling of an early Romanesque church.

At the other end of the gulf there is the **Palazzo Gallio**, also called the "Castello", built by Cardinal Tolomeo Gallio in 1583-86 and designed by Pellegrino Tibaldi. After having hosted French and Spanish troupes it later became the site of the Upper Western Mountain Community of the Lario. In the 12th century the medieval castle was razed to the ground and the villa that exists today was built on a square foundation with four massive corner towers. The loggias that face the lake are wonderful and the walls around the garden incorporate the remains of the old building nicely. Inside there is a large two-storey great hall.

Between the two extremities of the gulf lie the homes of Gravedona with a little port and pier. Today the narrow streets that run perpendicular to the lake are a testimony to the medieval layout of the village.

Once again on the state road Via Regina, but still in the town, on the left there is a road that branches off and goes up to the **Livo** and **Liro** valleys. This is an itinerary of particular interest with one of the more notable landscapes of the upper lake. As you make your way up, the panorama widens and widens. Follow the signs for Peglio to a hairpin bend and not far off from the road on the right there is a parish church dedicated to San Eusebio. The most famous works of the so-called Fiammenghino produced while in Lario have been preserved here. It is on these very frescoes and tapestries the artist Gian Mauro della Rovere painted his self portrait close to the portrait of his beloved farm girl.

Beyond the church you will pass through the town of Peglio and continue your ascent through a vast and grassy area to reach Livo. This mountain village is characterized by its rustic architecture with

Pp from 55 to 57: **Domaso**

wood ledges and the facades of the homes decorated with numerous votive frescoes. Just past the town there is an old church dedicated to San Giacomo (built in the second half of the 1400's) near the cemetery. Once past the church you can continue your journey by car to the 17th century Sanctuary of the Madonna of Livo and then another 2 kilometres on a beaten path the Casniolo shelter. After, you can continue on foot along a trail that will take you to the old bridge over the Livo stream.

Resuming the original itinerary you will find yourself once again on the state road headed toward Sorico. Once past the national electric company station (ENEL) in Gravedona on the right, you will quickly reach **Domaso** with its old homes many of which face the small port.

Just a little further beyond, we suggest you deviate briefly to **Vercana**. From the square of the parish church there is an ample view of the lake with the mouth of the Adda and the pond in Piona and convent of the same name on the opposite shore. Once again on the lakeside road you will reach **Gera Lario** with a square shaded by old sycamores. The houses here are positioned along the state road. Before entering the town there is a short paved road on the left that leads to the hamlet of **Burano** that offers a beautiful view of the lake and of **Montemezzo**. The parish Church of **San Martino** dominates the lake with a panorama that opens onto the mouth of the Adda and the Pian di Spagna. Large satellite antennae have been placed here by the Telespace Station of the Lario. The interior of the church is one of the areas most frescoed with the *Giudizio universale* and the *Crocefissione* attributed to Aurelio Luini son of the famous Bernardino. A valuable fresco is *La battaglia di Murat* that depicts the triumph of the Catholic faith over Lutheran by Gian Mauro della Rovere also known as the Fiammenghino. Other adornments, notably the altar on the left, were donated by those who had emigrated to Sicily.

Resuming your journey along the carriageway from Gera Lario you will reach **Sorico**. It is an old fishing village built after 1532 when the Mera river overflowed destroying the old town of Olonio. Here the state road runs parallel to the Mera river then crosses it over a cement bridge. This is the beginning of the **Pian di Spagna (Plains of Spain)** which is a large prairie at the mouth of the **Valtellina** and Mera valleys. At one time this location was plagued by malaria and floods but was later improved following an initial attempt in 1890 by the beatified priest Luigi Guanella. This area owes its name to the Spanish military settlements of the 1600's that controlled the strategic position of this land, between the territory of the Lario and the exit towards the plains of the Valtellina and **Valchiavenna,** from Forte di Fuentes.

An appendage of Lake Como is **Lake Mezzola** (6 square kilometres) that has been declared a protected area by the Region of Lombardy where migrating birds can find refuge. At the northern extremity of this body of water rises the Oratory of **San Fedelino** that can only be reached via water. If you go straight from the bridge over the Mera river you will reach the Lecco-Sondrio state road. However, to get to Lake Mezzola you would have to turn left after the bridge until you cross the state road that leads to Chiavenna. This road, which runs parallel to the railway, coasts the west shore of Lake Mezzola. You will pass through the towns of San Fedele, Verceia and Campo to finally arrive at Novate. At Novate a road sign

P 58:
Pian di
Spagna and
the Oratory
of San
Fedelino

on the left will give you directions to Samolaco and indicates what underpass you should take.

Legend has it that in the 10th century a woman from Novate Mezzola in a dream had a vision of where the body of San Fedele, beheaded by decree of Emperor Massimiliano in the year 286, had been buried. The bishop of Como was informed of this extraordinary vision according to which he would have to look for the relics of the martyr in the long forgotten mortuary chapel of a small church along the shores of the Mera river where it flows into Lake Mezzola. And so goes the story of the translation of the relics. In the year 964 the bishop of Como Ubaldo, "along with faithful followers boarded a ship lit with lamps and crossed the quiet lake to the oratory accompanied by hymns and songs. Upon finding the relics buried behind the altar he returned to Como with much festivity bringing them with him".

This is how it came to be that the old church in Como dedicated to Santa Eufemia changed its patron and was, and still is, dedicated to San Fedele. The small oratory on the Mera was named by the peo-

ple San Fedelino. No one knows if the legend is true but the fact remains that at the time the bishop of Como was having a hard time asserting his authority, even politically, which was being contested by his "colleague" in Coira. In the place where the relics of San Fedele were recovered a small church was built that is still there today. Probably in an attempt to make it clear that the area was indeed under him, the bishop of Como made sure that every inch of this little building was decorated in order to make it all the more precious in the eyes of the people of Como so that over time it would continue to be particularly well-loved by them. So goes the story of San Fedelino, real or presumed. The importance of this little monument lies in the fact that it is without a shadow of a doubt one of the most precious Romanesque pearls in Lombardy, be it for the building in itself or, simply, for the natural environment that houses it.

From San Fedelino, in order to return to Como quickly, you can take the state road n. 36 which by means of a series of tunnels is a fast way to Lecco. From here another throughway will take you to Como.

From Bellagio to Como
with a detour to Valassina

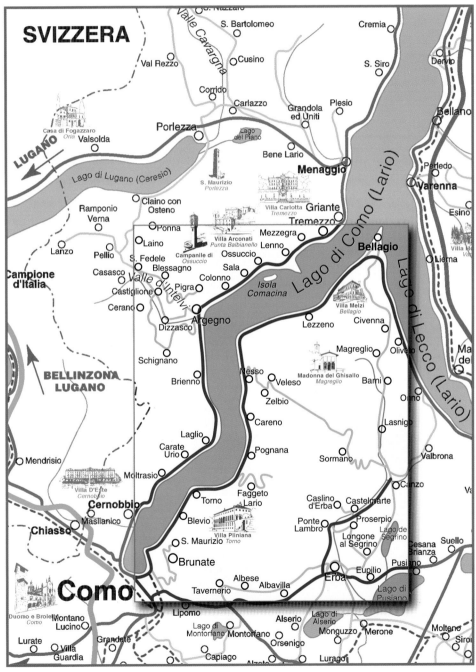

*Side: **Serbelloni hill, Bellagio***

P 65:
Villa
Melzi
and
gardens

Bellagio is one of the most famous tourist centres of the lake. Situated at the summit of the promontory that divides the Lario into the two branches of Como and Lecco, this city boasts famous villas with lush gardens. Along the lakeshore gallery there are elegant cafés and shops.

Upon entering the town, by way of Valassina, **Villa Serbelloni**, which currently belongs to the Rockefeller foundation, stands above on the right. It is host to cultural conventions and sojourns for study. History would have it that it rises from the very location were Pliny the Younger had once built his villa called "Tragoedia". The interior of the villa is made up of a series of halls with vaulted ceilings and decorations from the 17th and 18th centuries. Of greater interest is the extremely vast park that extends to the pinnacle of the promontory of Bellagio. It can be visited with the accompaniment of a guide twice daily at 11 a.m. and 4 p.m. from April 15 to October 15 except Mondays. It is

Villa
Serbelloni
above the
town of
Bellagio

certainly one of the most beautiful parks of Italy to be appreciated especially in autumn. Within are grottos, Italian styled gardens, traces of a Medieval wall and at the tip of the promontory the evocative panorama includes the remains of a little Romanesque church amid the ruins of the fortification. All of this is surrounded by secular plants and exotic cultivation.

Continuing beyond toward the village on the right there is the parish Church of San Giacomo full of works of art. Once past the road that crosses the length of the town you will descend to the lake and its lovely square with porticoes, elegant cafés and the pier for boats and hydrofoils. A little further ahead, the ferries that transport automobiles to the opposite shore leave.

Proceeding toward Como with the lake on your right, just minutes away from the pier, you will reach **Villa Melzi** where you can visit the gardens from March to October from 9 a.m. to 6:30 p.m. Before arriving at the villa you will cross a lush park created by modifying the terrain and the construction of imposing walls of support. Besides a majestic avenue of sycamore trees, holm-oak trees and rich azalea blooms, in the garden you can find various archaeological artefacts such as an Etruscan funeral urn, Egyptian, Roman and Greek sculptures as well as a small Moorish temple. It seems this temple was a favourite spot of **Liszt** who composed two pieces for piano right here in Bellagio. An elegant stairway leads to the villa which currently belongs to Gallarati Scotti. Next to the

*Pp from
66 to 71:*
Bellagio

dwelling there is a small museum and a little further ahead there is a chapel with the Melzi family funeral monuments.

From the south entrance of Villa Melzi you can quickly reach the small port of Loppia, where you can see another noble dwelling of the Lario, **Villa Trivulzio**, with a grand English styled garden. Further ahead there is yet another villa in neo-Gothic style with Moresque décor called **Villa Trotti**. Of particular interest is its park where, among other things there are plants from China and Japan. Leaving Bellagio behind you will now continue along a winding road past the hamlet of **San Giovanni** with a beautiful church of the same name. The road runs above the lake and offers lovely views of the opposite shore where there is Tremezzina and Villa Carlotta.

A panoramic spot toward Bellagio is the "**Punta della cappelletta**" that allows you to catch a lovely glimpse of the lake. At this point the view also opens onto Comacina Island and the first town you encounter is **Lezzeno** with its

seventeen hamlets either stretched out along the provincial road or clinging to the slopes of the mountain. You will encounter the following hamlets along the way: Villa, Sossana, Rozzo, Bagnana, Pescaù and Crotto. At the tip of Pescaù you can see a palace from the 1700's with a double archway that has recently been restored.

The road continues perpendicularly to the lake all the way to **Nesso.** At the entrance of the town, on the left, the road for the Pian del Tivano branches off to get to **Valassina** by crossing the Colma di Sormano.

Alternative route to Valassina. This is a detour that would be a shame to pass up. The winding road rises with a view of the lake that keeps getting wider. In the town of **Vico** there is the little Romanesque Church of Santa Maria with precious frescoes. You will now go through **Erno,** where metallic nets have been woven since the end of the 1600's, and arrive in **Zelbio** which is surrounded by magnificent woods. Nearby there are the grottos of Tacchi and of Zelbio. Veering off the road will lead you to **Veleso,** which is in a nice dominant position, while going straight on the hill will get less steep and take you to the large grassy basin of the **Pian del Tivano.** On the road that crosses the plateau the "Buco della Niccolina" opens up at its lowest point where the rain-water collected in the basin is poured out. Further ahead you will get to the **Colma di Sormano,** where you can admire the space observatory of Brianza as well as a very ample panorama of Sormano, Caglio and Rezzago with the Corni di Canzo in the background. At the top of the "Colma" there is the steep road that descends to Valassina which is dear to cyclists for the **Sanctuary of the Madonna del Ghisallo** wherein sou-

P 72:
Villa
Trivulzio,
Villa Trotti
and the
Church in
the hamlet
of San
Giovanni

Lezzeno

venirs of the greatest champions on two wheels are preserved. It is situated in Magreglio and can be reached by turning left along the road that from Erba, which is situated south between the cities of Como and Lecco, rises all the way to Bellagio.

P 74:
Sanctuary
of the
Madonna
del Ghisallo

Resuming your original route on the lake road, you will arrive in the town of **Nesso.** It is situated at the mouth of the Tuf and Nosè valleys from where streams descend from the Pian del Tivano to form a picturesque "**orrido**". Here the waters precipitate between the rocks in a beautiful cascade. This gorge is also visible from the small square along the provincial road or by going down from here along characteristic little streets and stairways to the lake where an old bridge joins the two shores of this course of water. Another option is to get there from the lake by boat. Above the town there are the remains of an old castle from the 14th century that was demolished by Francesco Sforza during the war against the Medeghino.

Pp 76
and 77:
Torno

The road continues mid-coast and after a deserted tract arrives at **Careno** which is a hamlet of Nesso and probably the most photographed town centre of the lake. It is a typical village in the form of a triangle. It is made up of stone houses clinging to the mountain along steep pathways that can only by reached on foot. The most important pathway starts at the level of the parish church and ends at the shore of the lake near the pier at the peak of the triangle. About a twenty minute

Careno

Villa
Pliniana

walk will take you to the top of the town, where there is the Masera grotto with a pond and a large hall that displays numerous ammonite fossils on the walls.

Continuing along the main route, staying on the high road above the lake, you will go through Pognana and Faggeto (in the hamlet of Palanzo there is a big wooden press from the 1500's that is still in perfect working condition).

The road will eventually start to descend and on the right there is the mountainside entrance to **Villa Pliniana,** which is currently privately owned, and then **Torno.** The town is situated in a nice position above a promontory right across from Moltrasio and stands out as a typical medieval village, which characteristics it has preserved to date despite the destruction it sustained in 1522 at the hands of the Spanish. Some of the houses are gathered around the Church of Santa Tecla and the beautiful little square on the lake with the pier. Other houses, however, can be found around the Church of San Giovanni further up the mountain. It is characterised by a beautiful Renaissance marble portal and is famous for having preserved to this day the relic of the Sacro Chiodo or "Sacred Nail" from the cross of Jesus.

Near San Giovanni is the start of the path that leads to Villa Pliniana (about 25 minutes on foot). This interesting building, which is not open to the public, owes its fame to an intermittent spring that from the top of the park takes a leap of about 80 metres. This beautiful cascade has been described by **Pliny the Elder** and **Pliny the Younger,** not to mention **Leonardo da Vinci.** The villa rises from the lake and is immersed in greenery. Giovanni Anguissola had it built in 1500 and hosted Foscolo, Rossini, Berchet, Stendhal, Shelley and Cristina Belgioioso.

From Torno a cartway branches off that leads to **Monte Piatto** (and passes by Piazzaga which is famous for its ancient tombs) where there is the "pietra pendula" or "pendulum stone", which is a prehistoric mass balanced on a rocky point, near the small church which honours Mary's visit to Elisabeth.

Once again on the provincial road, after just 2 kilometres and past the tunnel, you will reach **Blevio** with Villa Taglioni which belonged to the famous ballerina. In the cemetery rests the singer Giuditta Pasta (Ferranti chapel), for whom Bellini wrote *Sonnambula* and *Norma.* The most beautiful villas near the lakeside square at the boat wharf are: Cademartori, Da Riva and Pozzi. Before entering the town there is the famous Villa Taverna on the right with a park full of secular trees. Today it has been converted into condominiums.

Our itinerary has come to an end. The road now descends toward Como with a beautiful view. On the opposite shore appear Villa d'Este, Villa Erba and finally Villa Olmo. You will pass over the funicular that runs to Brunate and continuing down you will arrive in the city in the Sant'Agostino quarter.

Villa Taglioni

The Intelvi Valley

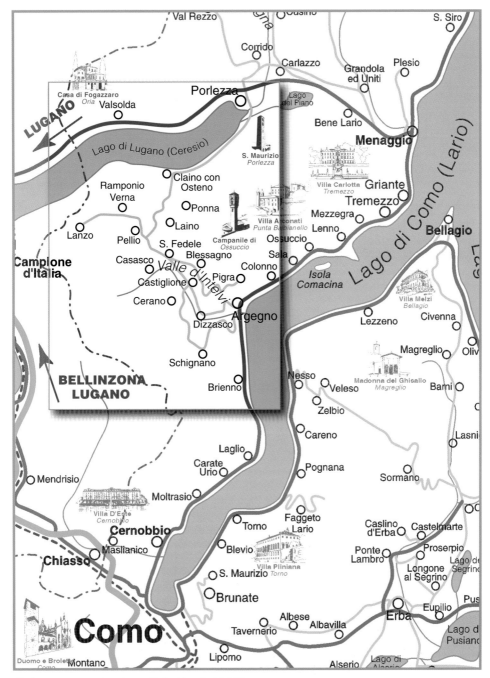

Side: **Panoramic view of the Intelvi Valley**

The **Valle Intelvi** is full of woods and fields with towns sown here and there. It is the ideal resort spot and connects Lake Como to Lake **Lugano**. The mountain slopes still give evidence of terraces created in past eras to recover land less steep in order to cultivate cereals, especially grain and rye. The "Maestri Comacini" were born in this valley and to this day many inhabitants of the area find work abroad, especially in Switzerland, as stonemasons, painters and plasterers.

Our itinerary starts off in **Argegno** right at the mouth of the valley. Not far from the fork where the road that leads to the valley branches of from the state road Regina there is the cable car station for **Pigra**.

Cable car in Pigra

Going up toward San Fedele, every bend in the road offers an ever greater view of the lake and Comacina Island. Once past Muronico you will arrive shortly in Dizzasco. Almost at the end of the town a cobblestoned road downhill (which you can drive on) leads to Telo stream where, near a humpbacked bridge, there are the remains of one of the few water mills still visible.

Continuing toward San Fedele a delightful panorama of the valley expands. Just before **Castiglione Intelvi**, a little below street level, there is the small Church of the "Madonna del Restello" built in 1717 on the left. It owes its name to the fact that in

this very location the inhabitants of the valley erected a barrier ("rastrelada" in the local dialect) to prevent the inhabitants from the lower valley from entering, thus defending themselves from the terrible plague epidemic which had been reaping victims everywhere. To visit inside you need to ask the high priest of Castiglione for the keys. Within you can see frescoes by **Giulio Quaglio** (1736), stuccoes and staggered frontals (a local product) and a Rococo altar.

Retegno, a hamlet of Schignano

From Castiglione turn left to get to Cerano at the foot of Mount S. Zeno. At the top (1'025 metres) there are the remains of the Romanesque church of the same name erected by the Magistri Intelvesi (Master Craftsmen of Intelvi).

Proceed to **Schignano** which like Cerano is a much appreciated resort town with vast prospects of the lake and many possibilities for mountain excursions on Parabello, Sasso Gordona, Grigno and Mount Comana. Schignano is famous for its carnival that takes place the Saturday and Tuesday before Ash Wednesday.

San Fedele

Pp 84 and 85: Argegno and the Intelvi Valley

Once back at Castiglione, go up the valley to **San Fedele Intelvi** positioned on a wide plateau, on the gulf between the Lario and Switzerland. Along with Lanzo, San Fedele is the most important centre of the valley.

This itinerary calls for you to continue toward Porlezza but at least three different trips that you can take from San Fedele must not be overlooked. Therefore, before continuing with the main itinerary, we will take a moment to consider these detours and the specific features of each one of them.

Variation 1: Pigra-Boffalora-Ponna

From the square in San Fedele pass right next to the parish Church of Sant'Antonio and at the entrance of a lane on the right follow the directions to Pigra. The road immediately rises and goes through the towns of Lura and Blessagno, with views of the Intelvi valleys first and then of Lake Como. Then there is **Pigra** with the station of arrival of the funicular that leaves from Argegno. This is a popular summer vacation spot. At a height of 779 metres above San Fedele you are now at an altitude of 882 metres and the air, even in the height of summer, is cool and crisp.

The left branch of the fork at the beginning of the town is the road to **Boffalora**. The first bend in the road above the town opens onto a magnificent view of the lake, the Grigne and Comacina Island. At another fork there are signs that give directions to Monte Galbiga. Please keep in mind that it is an old military road without guardrails or any other type of protection but, nevertheless, a paved easy road that is of great interest for the landscape. From Pigra there are another 6 kilometres to reach the Boffalora shelter

Pigra

(1'250 metres). The area is very panoramic and is characterized by vast pastures with watering holes for cattle. There is also a snack bar.

From Boffalora yet another fork in the road. Take the right and you will go up Monte Galbiga (you can also go by car but the road is not paved) all the way to the Venini shelter where you can still see the remains of trenches dug by soldiers during the First World War.

If you take the left you will descend toward the Alps of Tellero and the town of **Ponna**. Continuing in this direction, just beyond the fork, the road is unpaved for a couple of kilometres which poses no problem, however, for the motorist. Continue along a carriageway that unfolds through shady woods which is the ideal spot to stop if you are planning a relaxing picnic. Eventually you will arrive at the Alps of Tellero where there are also grassy fields and a watering hole for animals.

The road continues to descend and becomes more narrow. At the provincial road turn left to reach Laino and the road that leads to San Fedele on one side and Osteno on the other. Both locations are the main destinations of the itinerary but it would truly be a shame not to visit the town of Ponna which is divided into three hamlets: an upper, a middle and a lower.

If you decide to follow our advice to visit Ponna please be careful as the road there is rather narrow. Once at upper Ponna, in Piazza Ugo Ricci go up the short narrow steep road on the right *Boffalora* and at the top turn left. Resist the urge to take the level road on the right and go toward the washtub in front of you without allowing yourself to be intimidated by the decline. There will be a parish church

a little ahead. From the churchyard you can enjoy a beautiful panorama of Laino, Ramponio and Verna as well as catch a glimpse of Lake Lugano. Continue down the steep narrow little road until you reach a wider one. Turn right and follow the directions for lower Ponna and from this road you will have more views of Lake Lugano and Valsolda.

You will reach lower Ponna right near the Church of San Gallo e Desiderio of Romanesque origin but, like many other churches in the valley, was expanded in 1600. The dramatic facade was frescoed in the middle of 1700 and just before it there is the Via Crucis with chapels built in 1756 and decorated in 1771.

To continue, go down "Via 12 gennaio 1958". This date is of no particular importance in national history but is significant to the inhabitants of the area. In fact, on January 12, 1958 the inhabitants of lower Ponna who were fed up with being isolated took it upon themselves to build a road without waiting for permission from the public authorities. This very road, albeit difficult to travel, gave the inhabitants of Ponna access to medical care and all the other conveniences that a road like this would contribute to a community.

Continue going down and from the valley basin, after an equally steep ascent, you will arrive at San Fedele-Osteno. Turn left and after about a couple of kilometres there is Laino and then

San Fedele a little further ahead. Turn right here and proceed in the direction of Osteno and Lake Ceresio to pick up the original itinerary.

Variation 2: Casasco-Orimento-Erbonne
From the centre of San Fedele continue in the direction of Lanzo Intelvi and before exiting the town on the left the directions for Casasco-Erbonne can be clearly seen. Once at **Casasco**, the

Panoramic view of Pian d'Alpe in Casasco

road to the Orimento-Capanna Bruno shelter branches off on the right. The paved road rises quickly opening out onto new views of the valley and San Fedele. The area lends itself to relaxing picnics especially for the person wishing to escape the summer heat of the plains. Past Bolla with its large meadows there are the Grand Alps and finally **Orimento** (1'280 metres) where there is still the characteristic "nevera" or natural icebox. Here snow would be collected during winter months to conserve alpine products such as cheese, butter and fresh meat. Inside, the icebox is dug out deep into the earth in the form of a funnel and would usually be located in the shade of large trees.

View from Orimento

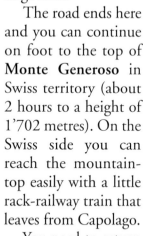

The road ends here and you can continue on foot to the top of **Monte Generoso** in Swiss territory (about 2 hours to a height of 1'702 metres). On the Swiss side you can reach the mountain-top easily with a little rack-railway train that leaves from Capolago.

You need to return to Casasco now. When you get on the road to Erbonne you will go through all the little villages which, like all the valley centres, have very narrow streets. Once through the villages the little centre of **Erbonne** is 6 kilometres away. Midway, the woods on the left side of the valley are in Swiss territory. On this excursion the views are ever-changing and look out onto Lake Como and Comacina Island. At Erbonne the carriageway ends and there are only pedestrian paths to Switzerland. Therefore you have to go back to Casasco. If you would like to go to Argegno on the opposite side of the Intelvi valley, at the exit to Casasco, you will find a road downhill on the right shaded by tall trees that will take you back to the lakeshore.

Variation 3: San Fedele-Lanzo-Sighignola summit

Start at the centre of San Fedele and go toward **Lanzo**. Ignore the turn-off for Casasco on the left and the one for Lake Lugano on the right and proceed straight until you reach Pellio Intelvi which is divided into a lower and an upper hamlet.

Pellio Inferiore (750 metres) is a splendid valley town with a great view of Ceresio and Porlezza. In an old castle here, noted bust sculptor Ercole Ferrata was born in 1610. He was the most famous of the "Magistri Intelvesi" and he has been attributed with the statuettes of the six Saints and with the Madonna del Rosario carved in wood with superb elegance. The old Church of San Michele preserves a tabernacle from 1500, various paintings from the Intelvi valley and on the front a fresco by Carlo Scotti of Laino. In the hamlet of Garello rises the oratory of the Madonna del Fiume with a statuette by Ferrata and a recently discovered fresco from 1500.

In **Pellio Superiore** there is the Romanesque Church of the Madonna di Caravaggio with stuccoes, statues and a few tapestries by Carlo Carloni. Of notable interest is the elegant 17th century Rococo ambiance of the vestry. From here you can get to Lanzo by passing through the "Pian delle noci" or "Walnut Plains" but this itinerary calls for you to proceed from lower Pellio to Lanzo.

The road descends toward the Telo river and offers nice views of the lake and valleys. Just after the bridge there is a turn-off for Ramponio and Verna which are two little towns with narrow streets characteristic of the valley.

From Verna you can proceed to **Lanzo** along a narrow but easily travelled road. Just outside of the town, at a bend, a path branches off that will take you to the aedicule of the "Madonna della bandiera" so named by the soldiers posted here during the First World War. Take note of the view from here that takes in the towns and mountains of Valsolda, the mountains of the Cavargna valley as well as Lake Piano. Continue by car to reach the restored little Church of "Sant'Antonio ai monti". This road, albeit awkward, lets you enjoy new and different sights of the valley below.

Once again on the main road that you left behind after the bridge over the Telo turn right in the direction of Lanzo and the first town you will encounter is **Scaria**. It still preserves much testimony to its prestigious history and it is no wonder that the "Museo della Valle Intelvi" (Diocese museum of art from the Intelvi valley) is located right in Scaria. Instituted in 1966, it is home to artefacts that bear testimony to both religious and secular life and culture of the people of the valley. Besides the museum, Scaria boasts a Romanesque church from the 12th century dedicated to Santi Nazzaro e Celso which is decorated with frescoes from the 1500's that are still well preserved.

Church of San Pancrazio in Ramponio

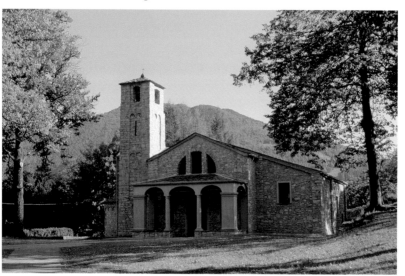

Among the citizens who have contributed the most to the fame of this location are the noble De Allio and Carloni families. The former, a family of ancient descent, acquired its stamp of nobility from Ferdinand of Austria through Domenico, the Imperial architect. His is the Palace of the Cavalry in Graz (the Landhaus). The most famous member of the family however is without a doubt Donato Felice whose signature is on the convent of Klosterneuburg not far from Vienna. From the Carloni family the most notable members are Giovan Battista and his sons Diego and Carlo. The father is the creator of the "carloneschi" style of strong stucco work. The strong contrast of this style of plastering does not take away from the architectural lines of the building but actually adds a harmonious decorative embellishment. The son Diego, also a plasterer, is the author of valuable works housed in Germany (Weingarten) and Genoa (Santa Maria di Carignano). The younger son Carlo Innocenzo on the other hand is a famed painter. He worked in Venice under another Intelvi valley native Giulio Quaglio di Laino. He later worked on the Cathedral of Lubiana in Einsiedeln, Switzerland and on the church of the Court of Ludwigsburg. Other works of his are in Mantova, Como and Milan.

Back on the provincial road go uphill to **Lanzo Intelvi**. This road coasts an important tourist centre with hotels and sports facilities and numerous villas from the late 1800's. On the upper part of the square stands the parish Church of San Siro. From Garibaldi square, go along Via Volta to get to the oratory of the Madonna di Loreto built in 1673 by Pietro Spazzi of Laino with a fresco in the portico by Carlo Carloni.

In Lanzo be sure not to miss the magnificent lookout onto Lake

Bridge over Lake Ceresio from Sighignola

Lugano toward Porlezza as well as the one about 6 kilometres from the town centre on the summit of **Sighignola**. The latter is called the "balcony of Italy" (1'300 metres) and can be reached by taking a well paved road that runs above the cities of Lugano and Capolago below. On nice days the view opens out onto Ceresio, Varesotto and the alpine chain from Monviso all the way to Jungfrau.

After Lanzo the carriageway continues on level ground and at

Lugano as seen from Sighignola

the end of a long avenue of trees separates into two directions. On the left it goes toward the **Pian delle noci** (campsite and golf course) from where you can go back to Argegno along the opposite side of the valley from where you went up. On the right there is the Italian-Swiss border not far off. Past the Italian border crossing

the road enters the Val Mara descending rapidly with narrow bends. The Swiss customs is at the bottom. By continuing on you will reach Campione d'Italia, a small piece of Italian land on Swiss soil.

Resuming the description of the main itinerary that was inter-

rupted in San Fedele Intelvi, leave it behind and head in the direction of Lanzo and at the roundabout follow the directions for Osteno-Porlezza. The road will begin to descend through the town of Laino which is the birthplace of many artists. At the end of the lane between the houses you will arrive at the parish Church of San Lorenzo which is preceded by an arch from the old retaining wall of the churchyard. Inside the church is one of the most complete examples of Baroque décor in the valley.

The provincial road continues downhill toward the Italian branch of **Lake Lugano** which is also called **Lake Ceresio**. Go past the junction of the little road from Ponna, and go past the towns of Barclaino and Claino on the right to get to **Osteno** valley at the end. Before entering the town, on the left you will find the entrance of an evocative cascade that can be visited via boat. It is a long and deep gorge carved out of the rock by the Telo stream that ends in a rumbling waterfall. In Osteno the little square on the lake is also unique.

Church of San Maurizio

The road continues on level ground along the lake. Past the wa-

terfall on the right you will reach the **Grotte di Rescia** shortly. These are small caverns with stalactites and stalagmites created by the erosive action of water and calcium. These grottos are open to the public from Easter to September from 2 p.m. to 6 p.m. (paid entry).

Further ahead, before the straight stretch that leads to **Porlezza**, near the Galbiga grotto a small beaten path leads to the **Church of San Maurizio** which was buried by an avalanche in 1300 but later uncovered in 1956 by volunteer workers.

At the end of the straight stretch that crosses the plains of Porlezza turn right to get to Lake Como and Menaggio. If you turn left you will go toward Lugano from where you can take the highway to Chiasso and get to Como quickly.

The Intelvi Valley

From Menaggio to Porlezza
Cavargna and Rezzo valleys including Valsolda

Side: Menaggio and the Upper Lake as seen from "La Crocetta" lookout

At the beginning of the town of **Menaggio** at the intersection with the traffic lights leave the lakeshore state road and follow the directions to Porlezza-Lugano. The road immediately rises up the mountain with sharp turns. Go past the turn-off on the right for Loveno, a hamlet of Menaggio, famous for its villas and from where a panoramic road that goes up to Plesio and Breglia has got a lookout that offers a lovely view of the Lecco branch of the Lario. Continue uphill past the turn-off for the local hospital and follow the road to Porlezza. You will pass Croce, another hamlet of Menaggio, with a golf course. Just past the top of the hill you will enter the towns of Grandola and Uniti.

Cardano

Instead of proceeding straight along the state road, which is the fastest way to Porlezza, Lugano and Como, you will find it much more interesting to turn right and follow the directions to **Grandola** and **Uniti**. This way you will travel along a road that runs parallel to the state road but much higher up the slopes of the mountains offering a greater view. The towns you will pass through are also interesting. Not far from the intersection there is a fork in the road. The right turn leads to the first town **Cardano** which is about 100 meters away. As with the other town centres in the valley it is true to its medieval roots with rural courtyard houses. In the small square of the town rises Villa Bagatti-Valsecchi (early 1900's) with a large park facing the Senagra valley below. You can visit the park only by appointment. The pleasantness of this place is well described in the following inscription found outside one of the houses in the little square: "O passeggier che vieni di lontano, ristorati un momento al bel Cardano"("Oh wanderer come from a distance, rest in lovely Cardano for an instance").

To continue your outing you have to go back to the fork and turn right following the directions, in the order that you will encounter them, for Gonte, Codogna, Velzo, Naggio and Monti di Gottro.

The paved road starts to rise higher and higher treacherously. Go through Codogna, which is the site of the town hall for many of the hamlets that make up the towns of Grandola and Uniti, and then through Velzo and Naggio. At this point you will go around a parish church on the left and just a little ahead there will be a fork. Take the left road and follow the directions to Gottro. The road now proceeds downhill through woods and fields giving you a beautiful view of the plains of Porlezza below as well as Lake Piano and Lake Lugano.

At the beginning of the town of **Gottro**, a hamlet of **Carlazzo**, there is a well marked street on the left that leads to the Romanesque basilica of **San Giorgio** (12th century). In order to visit the inside you have to ask the priest for the keys. The monument is about a kilometre away and is surrounded by a small cemetery. In any case, you can admire the interesting frescoes inside through the windows out front next to the entrance door. Proceeding along, shortly thereafter you will encounter another fork in the road. Turn left and go downhill along a wider carriageway to **Carlazzo**.

At this point you have two possible itineraries to choose from. The first is to continue toward Porlezza. If you choose to go in this direction, at the intersection with the provincial road first turn right then turn left and follow the directions to Corrido. You will get there by crossing the high bridge called the "Saltone" that goes over a ravine at the bottom of which runs the Cuccio stream. You will reach Vesetto from where you turn left to get to Porlezza.

The alternative itinerary would have you take the route that rises along the Cavargna valley and then goes down the Rezzo valley to eventually pick up where the other itinerary left off at Vesetto. This detour is recommended for the special mountain features it offers. The proposed road is completely paved but the descent into Rezzo valley is very narrow. From Carlazzo follow the directions for Cusino-San Bartolomeo Val Cavargna and go up the Pidaggia mountainside. On the right side of the road in the middle of a field there is the Church of Sant'Ambrogio of the 13th century believed to be the oldest in the valley. Further ahead there is Cusino and then **San Bartolomeo** which is the most important centre. It has got a grand parish church of the same name with

Pp 102 and 103: Bellagio from "La Crocetta" lookout above Menaggio

Cavargna

marble altars and staggered frontals. After there is **San Nazzaro** that has a beautiful view overlooking Cusino. You will then arrive in **Cavargna** (1'071 metres), the capital of this valley. Besides the wonderful natural environment of this location submersed in woods that protect the town from avalanches, there is also the Museo della Valle an ethnographic museum open Sundays from 2 p.m. to 5 p.m. It contains a comprehensive documentation of activities in the valley of old including iron metallurgy and the mining industry that was once very active in this area but has long since disappeared. That very industry probably gave birth to the occupations that, throughout the last century, made the people of this territory known throughout the plains of Lombardy. Tradesmen such as blacksmiths and tinsmiths would make house calls to line copper pots with tin in order to make them suitable for cooking. From here you can continue going up a less comfortable road than before to reach the pastures of Vegna with only cattle herds to keep you company. Otherwise go in the direction of the Rezzo valley to quickly reach Buggiolo where the road that leads to Seghebbia, the highest town in the valley (1'150 metres) branches off. Going down, however, you will encounter vast panoramas (the most spectacular being the chapel of Scaleta) on your way to Corrido with its little hamlets. Then there is Molzano and Bicagno. Finally you will reach Vesetto where you can pick up with the road to the original itinerary destination of Porlezza.

Porlezza is a modern tourist town situated at the northern extremity of Lake Lugano (also called Lake Ceresio) surrounded by many well-equipped campsites that stretch out along the coast of the plains of Porlezza toward Osteno.

The itinerary heads to Switzerland along a narrow and winding road amid greenery and mountainsides sewn with little villages, every one of them deserving of a visit.

Leaving Porlezza behind take the tunnel that appears right in the town centre on the lake to reach **Cima** which is also a nice lakeshore shaded by large trees. The houses here create a backdrop to the street with the occasional interruption of little lanes that rise toward the mountains.

From Cima you will enter the territory of Valsolda which is a short picturesque valley that extends all the way to the Swiss border. Sandwiched between the lake and the rugged dolomite mountains, the area is protected to the north by the Alpine mountain

Pp 106 and 107: Lake Piano (foreground), Porlezza and Lake Ceresio (background)

Porlezza

chain. To the south a barrier of morainal hills protects it from the fog of the Padana plains. The "breva", a local term used to describe the breeze that blows on afternoons from the south to the north helps, along with the lake water mass, to lessen the summer heat and to create a more healthy and clean atmosphere. The presence of olive trees is a clear indication of the mild climate of this area.

This is an area that, under the protection of the archbishop of Milan, managed to maintain its independence for a long time from Charlemagne up until May 15, 1783. On May 15 of that year by means of the falsification of old documents and through legal loopholes (against which the archbishop of the time, the noble Milanese Filippo Visconti, "more pious than powerful", could not stand up) this part of Italy fell under the Austrian empire which managed to impose its unfair taxes on it .

Beyond Cima, just above the state road is the Sanctuary of **Nostra Signora della Caravina** erected in 1662 in a beautiful position where there once stood another built in 1570. From the churchyard, which can be reached by car, there is a nice view of the lake

Valsolda

with the town of Osteno in front and Claino a little above. In the back is Gandria, the "Paradise" of Lugano and Mount San Salvatore. Just a little way from the yard of the sanctuary there is a little temple dedicated to San Carlo.

Past the hamlet of Cressogno, through a short tunnel there is the turn off on the right for Loggio, Drano, Puria and Dasio. These are other hamlets that dot the **Valsolda**. The ones on high are the oldest and are connected by mule track, but today can also be reached by car thanks to the lake road that dates back to the turn of the last century.

Now there is Drano and then Puria whose most illustrious citizen is Pellegrino Tibaldi, sculptor and architect already well known when, thanks to the patronage of Cardinal Carlo Borromeo, he was nominated architect of the city and of the government of Milan. He later abandoned his many local responsibilities to go to Spain to serve Filippo II and work on El Escorial. He returned to Milan in 1696 "with a sack load of money" and the title of Marquis to lord it over "his native land". Above Puria, finally there is Dasio, a starting point for many excursions.

Again on the state road continue to **San Mamete** with the spectacular little square that opens onto the lake and from where extremely narrow and pretty lanes branch off.

The itinerary proceeds passing by **Albogasio** where on the south side of the parish church, on a promontory at the edge of the lake, you can still see the crests of the archbishops of Milan who had them painted in symbol of their sovereignty here. Finally you will reach **Oria**.

This is the heart of an area tied up with the story of **"Piccolo Mondo Antico"** the masterpiece by **Antonio Fogazzaro** an author

Oria

of the 1800's who like Manzoni deserves to be remembered in the literary history of Como. The plot of the novel is set in this location between 1852 and 1859 at the conclusion of great political events and the dawn of others as Italy prepares to emerge as a nation. Despite all this the little world of Valsolda remains "quiet, miserable and tranquil". Fogazzaro's secondary characters were inspired by real people whom he described with kind indulgence and a sense of humour. Many public places here are named after the characters in the book, particularly Ombretta the little girl who drowns in the dock of the villa where the main characters live.

Continuing toward the Swiss border the road for **Castello** branches off on the right. This is probably the most characteristic of the town centres of the valley. It is worth a brief stop over to visit it, if not only for the panoramic views of the lake that you can catch sight of along the road. This town was built in relatively recent times and perhaps due to the fact that it remains isolated it has managed to maintain a uniqueness with notes of a past nobility testified by the portals of the houses that look onto the little streets.

Back on the state road, before crossing the border, we suggest you park your car in the little lot on the left. On the other side of the road, go down the steps that lead to the entrance of a villa from where you go down another stairway to the lake. You will arrive at a little square facing Lake Cersio with **Villa Fogazzaro** on one side and the little Church of San Sebastiano on the other. This is the ideal spot for a relaxing stroll. Go through the tunnel of the

Campione d'Italia

villa to get to the garden, mentioned often in Fogazzaro's novel, and to the famous dock where Ombretta drowns in pursuit of her little boat. The dwelling which currently belongs to Marquis Roi, the writer's nephew, is not open to the public.

If, however, you decide to go in the opposite direction at the square toward Oria, you will be able to appreciate the tranquillity and beauty of the landscape just as well.

A little cluster of houses on the other side of the lake is part of the territory of Valsolda Santa Margherita and can only be reached by boat.

To get to **Campione d'Italia** you need to cross the Italian-Swiss border. Once past the Italian customs you will go through a tunnel before arriving at the Swiss customs. After the usual formalities of border crossing you will be in the city of **Lugano** where you

will go along the beautiful lakeshore and then take the county road
n. 2. A long bridge (816 metres), under which boats pass, crosses
Lake Lugano. Just before the bridge on the right there is the **Suisse
Miniature** theme park that is home to models to scale of the most
important monuments and mountains in Switzerland.

Once over the bridge, turn left and after about 3 kilometres a
large arch marks the entrance to **Campione d'Italia**. This is the
homeland of the architects, sculptors and stone cutters known as
the "Maestri Campionesi" who conducted a thriving business in
Italy and abroad between the 12th and the 14th centuries.

Campione has continued to be Italian land on Swiss soil following the donation of this territory to the Monastery of Sant'Ambrogio of Milan in the 7th century. When the valleys of Ticino
passed from the hands of the duchy of Milan to the Confederation
of Helvetica the land belonging to the convent was not included.
It was only after the abolition of religious orders by Napoleon
(1797) that the territory of Campione was joined to the district
of Lario. This peculiarity can still be noted in juridical, adminis-
trative and fiscal matters as well as in civil life. The currencies used
here are indiscriminately the Swiss franc and the Euro. The **Casinò
Municipale** of Campione d'Italia is open everyday (except Decem-
ber 24 and 25) from 10:30 a.m. to 5 a.m. and Fridays and Satur-
days until 6 a.m. You must present valid identification in order to
access the gambling hall.

Once through the arch that marks the border between Switzerland and the Italian territory of Campione, keep to the right to
go through the upper part of the town and get to the square on
the lake. The former Church of Zenone is now the town's civil art
gallery with significant works by the Maestros of Campione from
the 1300's and 1400's. Past the walkway along the lake in the
square you will then return to the arch. On the right there is the
Sanctuary of the Madonna dei Ghirli (Madonna of Swallows)
with a dramatic stairway that descends from the facade to the lake.
Under the portico there are frescoes from 1514 (Universal Judgement, Hell, The story of Adam and Eve). The interior is also decorated with the Story of the Virgin, the sequence of months and
other valuable paintings.

Lecco and the east side of the lake up to Colico with the Lecco-Bellagio detour

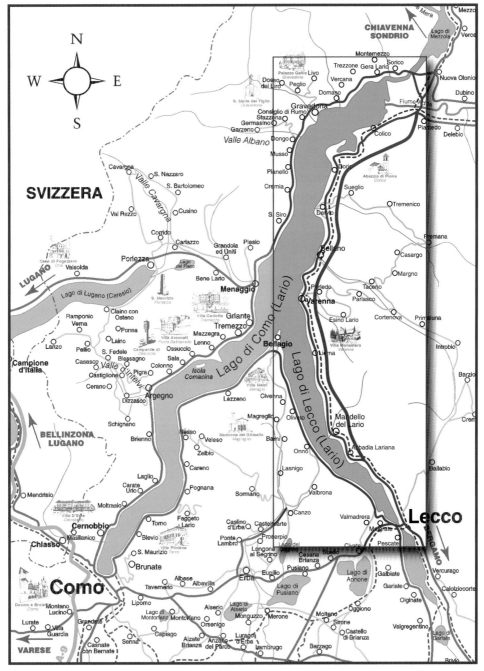

Side: **partial view of Varenna**

P 115:
Basilica of
San Nicolò
and Piazza
Cermenati

The city of **Lecco** lies at the southern extremity of the east branch of Lake Como. The provincial capital since 1992, it is a city of Roman origin protected by the imposing outline of **Mount Resegone**. Formerly known as "Leuco", in medieval times it was fortified by strong surrounding walls later destroyed toward the end of 1700.

Pp 116
and 117:
Lecco

The symbol of this industrious city is no doubt the **Ponte Visconteo**, or Ponte Vecchio, a bridge that goes over the Adda river at the point where it flows out of the lake to continue its course toward the plains. The bridge was built by Azzone Visconti between 1336 and 1338 who had a tower placed at either end. These towers were equipped with drawbridges that could transform the construction into a sort of fortress as need be.

The historical town centre is concentrated on the lakeshore and in the picturesque squares that lie adjacent to a beautiful and fascinating promenade. You will start your visit in the **Piazza Cermenati** with typical merchant homes as well as the "fear inspiring" **Palazzo della Paura** where taxes were collected. From here rises the Basilica dedicated to **San Nicolò** with a high neo-Gothic bell tower that reaches a height of 96 metres. The church was built upon the remains of the medieval walls and to this day is home to the relics of the pa-

Lecco

tron saint of sailors and boat-
men. Behind the square there
are the narrow lanes that at one
time made up the commercial
part of the city and then there
is the historic Piazza XX set-
tembre which was remodelled
in 1800. Between the houses it
is possible to catch a glimpse of
the old **Torre Viscontea**, now a
museum, which once belonged
to the castle destroyed along
with the city walls in the 18th
century. Now go to Piazza
Garibaldi where there is the
Neoclassical Teatro della Soci-
età as well as buildings from the
1900's such as the Justice
building by Rationalist architect Cereghini.

Piazza Manzoni however is host to the monument
of the famous writer **Alessandro Manzoni**. He described this branch of Lake Como in his well known
novel "**I Promessi Sposi**", making these places familiar
to entire generations. On the same square you can admire the Sanctuary of Nostra Signora della Vittoria
erected in memory of the soldiers who died during the
First World War.

The 18th century **Villa Manzoni,** also called Cale-
otto, houses much testimony to the life of the famous
writer who spent most of his childhood here. It is currently home to the "Manzoniano" museum where you
can find manuscripts and mementos from the life and
works of the most important citizen of Lecco.

Then there is Castello, an elegant neighbourhood of
Lecco, with Palazzo Belgioioso of the 1700's which is
also a museum. Also at the gates of the city there is the
pretty village of **Pescarenico**. The part that lies along
the lake still has the imprint of a typical fishing village
where is seems time has stood still.

Villa Monastero

The landscape of this area is really magnificent. High mountains surround the lake - the very mountains that Manzoni described as 'springing forth from the waters' in his novel "I Promessi Sposi". Along the side of the Lario, rising north, are the dolomite mountaintops of the **Grigne** which have always been a trekker's and climber's paradise. These mountains frame the green valleys, such as Valsassina, beautifully and are hot spots for winter sport.

Lecco-Bellagio Variation

After visiting Lecco the itinerary calls for you to continue along the lake in the direction of Colico. It is worthwhile, however, to consider a variation that could be an interesting alternative along the left shore of the branch of the lake in Lecco that runs along the state road 583 that connects Lecco to

Pp 120 and 121: Varenna

Bellagio. This tract is called the "olive coast" for the many olive groves
that were once characteristic of the area but have all but disappeared
now.

You will immediately encounter **Malgrate** with its pretty little

*Pp 122
and 123:
Panormic
view of
Vezio
Castel*

port. Then go through a tunnel to reach **Oliveto Lario** about a couple kilometres away made up of the lovely lakeside hamlets of Onno, Vassena and Limonta which are popular in the summer for their little beaches. In Limonta the Sanctuary of the Madonna del Moletto, situated vertically on the lake is of particular interest. Inside there are priceless frescoes from the 1600's.

After a few kilometres you will reach Bellagio, the pearl of Lake Como. Here you can pick up with itinerary n. 2 that goes down all the way to Como.

*Waterfall
(Orrido)
in Bellano*

The main itinerary, however, leads along the right shore of the branch of the lake in Lecco. Go out of the city of Lecco, take the new motorway n. 36 a short way and then the provincial road n. 72 which coasts the lake to reach **Abbadia Lariana** at the mouth of the Zerbo

stream. This pretty village owes its name to the Benedictine abbey that was built around the 9th century. Today only the cloister and a few frescoes remain. In the south of the village the **Torraccia**, an old medieval tower built to defend this tract of the lake, stands out.

The itinerary continues and immediately takes you to **Mandello del Lario** framed by the imposing mountaintops of the **Grigne**. The town centre still has typical medieval-looking houses with colonnades. Without a doubt the town owes its fame to the Guzzi motorbike factory where there is an interesting museum with over 100 limited edition models and racing bikes.

Continue along the coast road to reach **Lierna** built behind Monte Cuccio, full of villas and gardens. The upper part is dominated by the Church of S. Ambrogio, rebuilt in 1626 upon a previous religious edifice.

Not far off there is **Fiumelatte**, a bubbling stream that pours thunderously into the lake after a course of only 250 metres. It only flows during the period that runs from spring to autumn.

Surely, however, the most important town on this side of the Lario is **Varenna** in a magnificent position at the helm of the entire lake centre. There are the colourful fishermen's houses and a small port with a walkway that seems to be suspended over the water. There are also two wonderful and elegant villas. **Villa Monastero**, which lies within a grandiose park full of exotic plants, owes its name to the

Corenno Plinio

P 127:
The Abbey
in Piona

convent that existed here in the 1200's. Today the villa has been transformed into a centre for study and congress. The Neoclassical **Villa Cipressi** is in a unique position which dominates all of the lake centre. It is currently a hotel. In the upper part of the town rises the 12th century Church of San Giorgio with a high bell tower and interesting frescoes from the 1500-1600's. Also of note are the Churches of Santa Marta and Santa Maria both from the 1600's that face the main square.

Further up, in a dominant position is the famous **Castello di Vezio.** You can still see the tower and part of the castle wall.

Follow the itinerary to reach the town of **Bellano.** Strategically built at the mouth of the Valsassina it was one of the most important ports of the Lario. It lies amid tall cypress trees and is famous for the **orrido** which is an evocative waterfall of the Pioverna stream that pours into a deep gorge between the rocks. A visit to the waterfall is very exciting thanks to the narrow catwalks that hang vertically from the walls of the gorge.

The next town is **Dervio** with its old houses and elegant lakeshore built around the Varrone stream. The oldest town centre is **Corenno Plinio** which is a picturesque hamlet dominated by the medieval castle that protects the old houses with its large steps carved out of the rock.

Proceed along the coast to find Dorio, originally a farming village that today is made up of various hamlets built around numerous churches.

Just a little beyond, in a panoramic position at the end of the Olgiasca peninsula, you have **Piona** with its little lake. This location is known for the splendid 12th century Benedictine Abbey and the attractive cloister that dominates the bay with its 41 columns in white marble. This important religious complex is in the care of Cistercian monks who are famous for distilling excellent liqueurs and herbal infusions.

At this point you are on the border of the province of Sondrio and you can see **Colico** which lies silently at the foot of Monte Legnone (2'609 metres) the importance of which has increased little by little over the last decades due to its strategic position. Our itinerary ends here.

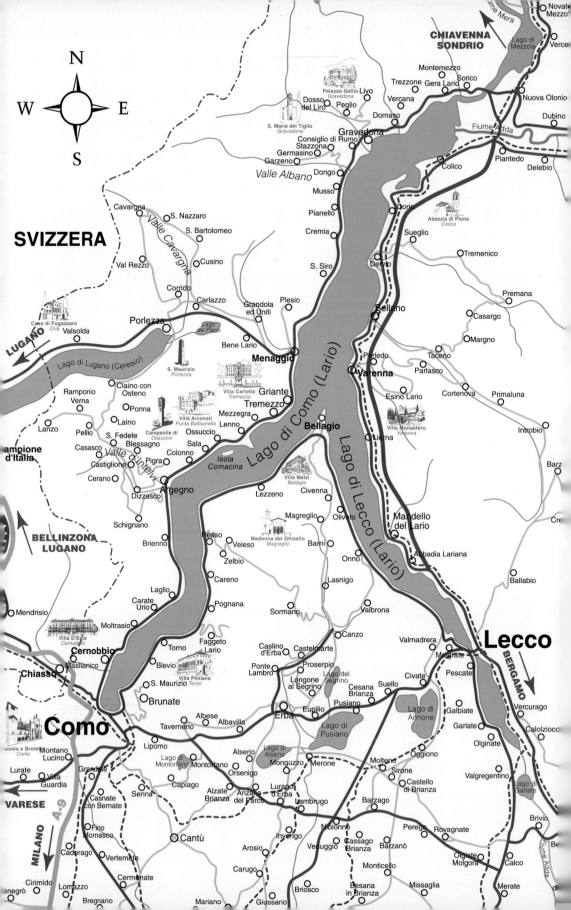